Whispers
of
Blessings

A 30-Day Devotional for a Grace-filled New Year

Whispers of Blessings
A 30-Day Devotional for a Grace-filled New Year

Scripture quotations are primarily taken from the **King James Version (KJV)** of the Holy Bible. Other translations may be used occasionally for clarity and are noted where applicable.

This devotional is intended for spiritual encouragement and personal reflection. It is not a substitute for professional counseling, pastoral care, or medical advice.

Cover Design: Hendia Minnis
Interior Layout & Design: Nadia Farrington
Edited by: Haeli Minnis
Published by: Nadia Farrington

www.whispersatsunrise.com

ISBN: 979-8-9930641-4-7

Printed in the United States of America.

Table of Contents

The Devotional Journey

Dedication

This devotional is dedicated to every heart entering a new year carrying both hope and heaviness, to the one standing at the threshold of a new beginning while still holding the weight of what has been.

To the soul believing God for more, more peace when the mind feels restless, more clarity when the path ahead feels uncertain, more healing where wounds are still tender, and more trust when faith feels fragile.

This is for those who are quietly pressing forward, praying soft prayers that may never be spoken aloud. For those who are learning that strength does not always roar, and faith does not always feel bold.

May these whispers remind you that God's blessings are not always loud or immediate. They are often gentle, unfolding slowly in moments of stillness, obedience, and surrender. And even when unseen, they are always present covering you, guiding you, and carrying you into what God has lovingly prepared for you.

May this year be one where you recognize His hand in the small things, feel His nearness in the quiet moments, and rest in the assurance that you are never walking alone.

Introduction

A new year often arrives with expectation of fresh goals, renewed faith, and quiet prayers whispered in hopeful anticipation. Yet it can also carry unspoken fears, lingering questions, and a desire for reassurance that God is still near and still working.

Whispers of Blessings was created as a gentle companion for your journey into the year ahead. Rather than rushing you forward, this devotional invites you to slow down and listen. To notice how God often speaks in soft moments through scripture, reflection, prayer and the quiet assurance of His presence.

Each day is designed to help you reflect, pray, and declare God's truth over your life. You will find encouragement for your faith, reminders of God's faithfulness, and space to record personal declarations that can be revisited throughout the year.

As you begin this journey, may you discover that blessings are not only found in answered prayers, but also in God's steady guidance, His nearness in uncertainty, and His grace that meets you daily.

How to Use This Devotional

This devotional is designed to be used daily, but it is also flexible enough to meet you where you are.

Each day includes:

- A **Scripture** to anchor your heart
- A **Devotional Reflection** to encourage deeper understanding
- A **Prayer** to guide your conversation with God
- A **Blessing Declaration** to speak God's truth over your life
- A **Personal Declaration** for you to write and revisit throughout the year

You may choose to read one day each morning, reflect in the evening, or return to specific days whenever your heart needs reassurance. There is no pressure to rush, allow this devotional to become a quiet space where you meet God consistently and honestly.

At the back of the book, you will find a **Personal Declaration Chart**, created to help you gather and revisit the words you've spoken in faith. These declarations can become prayers you return to throughout the year, reminding you of what God has spoken and what you are believing Him for.

Opening Prayer

Heavenly Father,

As I step into this new year, I invite You to lead me. Quiet my heart so I may hear Your voice. Teach me to recognize Your blessings, even when they come as gentle whispers. Strengthen my faith, steady my spirit, and help me trust You with what lies ahead. May this season be marked by grace, growth, and deeper dependence on You. I place this year in Your hands, knowing You are faithful. Amen.

Blessings for the Heart

This week invites you to slow down, breathe deeply, and let God speak to the tender places within your heart. Before He strengthens your hands or guides your steps, He first brings peace, renewal, and gentle restoration to the inner parts of your soul. As you move through these seven days, may your heart grow lighter, your spirit grow calmer, and your awareness of God's presence grow deeper. Let Him whisper healing, hope, and blessing into the quiet spaces within you.

DAY 1

A Whisper of New Beginnings

And he that sat upon the throne said, **Behold, I make all things new**. *And he said unto me, "Write: for these words are true and faithful."*

Revelation 21:5

There is something sacred about a new beginning. It doesn't ask you to strive or be perfect, it simply invites you to breathe. **Matthew 11:28 -30** reminds us that God does not demand striving He invites rest, relief, and gentleness. God meets you gently in the quiet places, ready to renew what feels worn and refresh what has grown weary. *Isaiah 40:29-31 "He gives power to the faint; and to them that have no might he increases strength."*

As you enter this new year, allow your soul to exhale. God is not measuring you by last year's struggles, **Isaiah 43:18-19** reminds us of this. His mercy has stepped ahead of you, preparing a soft place for your feet to land. He delights in giving you a fresh start, one filled with grace, peace, and gentle restoration.

> *Isaiah 43:18-19*
>
> *Remember ye not the former things, neither consider the things of old. Behold, I will do a new thing; now it shall spring forth; shall ye not know it? I will even make a way in the wilderness, and rivers in the desert.*

He specializes in renewal.
He restores what felt heavy.
He refreshes what grew weary.
He whispers hope into places you thought were forgotten.

You don't have to carry last year into this one. God is offering you a soft reset a new grace, a new strength, and a new peace that will follow you through every day of this year.

Prayer

Father, thank You for new beginnings. Whisper Your peace over my mind and heart. Help me release what no longer serves me and step into the new year with quiet confidence in Your love. Amen.

Blessing Declaration

I step into this year with grace, peace, and a heart open to God's renewal.

Personal Declaration (**Write Below**)

Today, I choose to begin again. I release _________________ and welcome _____________ into my life.

____

____

____

DAY 2

A Whisper of Favor

For thou, Lord, will bless the righteous; with favor will thou compass him as with a shield.

Psalm 5:12

God's favor is not loud. It doesn't need to be. It often arrives quietly opening a door you didn't expect, placing the right person in your path, or granting you a peace that makes no sense in the natural.

As you step into this year, trust that His favor is not something you earn; it is something you *walk in*. He surrounds you with it, goes before you with it, and strengthens you through it. You are not entering this year alone. **Psalm 84:11** paints a picture of God's favor going before us and covering us. *"For the Lord God is a sun and shield: the Lord will give grace and glory: no good thing will he withhold from them that walk uprightly."* Remember favor embraces you like a shield.

> *Isaiah 45:2*
>
> *I will go before thee, and make the crooked places straight: I will break in pieces the gates of brass, and cut in sunder the bars of iron:*

As you move through each day, let this assurance settle deeply within you: God's favor is not seasonal or selective it is steady, constant, and personal. It meets you in the ordinary moments and the unexpected ones, reminding you that you are seen, valued, and carried by His love. Even when circumstances feel uncertain, His favor is quietly working behind the scenes, arranging what you cannot yet see and preparing blessings that will unfold in His perfect timing.

Prayer

Father, let Your favor guide my steps this year. Lead me to the places You have prepared and let Your hand rest gently upon my life. May Your favor go before me and make the way clear. Amen.

Blessing Declaration

God's favor surrounds me. Doors open for me according to His purpose.

Personal Declaration (**Write Below**)

Today, I will walk confidently, trusting that God's favor is with me in

____

____

____

DAY 3

A Whisper of Peace

And the peace of God, which passes all understanding, shall keep your hearts and minds through Christ Jesus.

Philippians 4:7

Peace is not the absence of noise it is the presence of God. His peace rests gently over your life like a warm covering. It guards the places that feel fragile and settles the thoughts that try to run wild.

This year, let God's peace be your anchor. **Colossians 3:15 *And let the peace of God rule in your hearts*,** *to the which also you are called in one body; and be you thankful.* When worry rises, return to His presence. When fear whispers, turn your face toward Him. His peace is not momentary; it is a gift He continually pours into the heart that seeks Him.

> *Isaiah 26:3*
>
> *Thou wilt keep him in perfect peace, whose mind is stayed on thee: because he trusted in thee*

Let His peace settle over you like a soft covering, calming the thoughts that try to run ahead and steadying the places within you that feel uncertain. The peace God gives is not fragile it holds firm even when life shifts around you. As you yield your heart to Him, His peace will not only quiet your spirit but guide your steps, reminding you that you are never walking alone.

Prayer

Lord, let Your peace settle over my life today. Guard my heart, quiet my mind, and help me rest in Your presence. Teach me to release every worry into Your hands and to breathe deeply in the assurance of Your love. Let Your peace rule where anxiety once tried to lead and let Your calm fill every corner of my spirit. Draw me closer to You with each moment and let Your gentle whisper remind me that I am safe, held, and never alone. Amen.

Blessing Declaration

The peace of God guards my heart and mind. I receive His calm today.

Personal Declaration (**Write Below**)

Today, I choose peace over anxiety. I will trust God with

____

____

____

DAY 4

A Whisper of Strength

The Lord is my light and my salvation; whom shall I fear? **the Lord is the strength of my life**; of whom shall I be afraid?

Psalm 27:1

Some days strength arrives as a gentle whisper. Not in the form of loud courage, but in the quiet ability to get up, try again, forgive again, and keep walking forward. It's the steady resilience that rises when you thought you had nothing left to offer. **2 Corinthians 12:9** *And he said unto me, My grace is sufficient for thee:* ***for my strength is made perfect in weakness***. It's the grace that meets you in ordinary moments strength that doesn't demand attention but faithfully carries you through each day. God's strength often appears in subtle ways, reminding you that the smallest steps can still lead to the greatest victories.

> **Philippians 4:13**
>
> *I can do all things through Christ which strengthened me.*

God strengthens you from within. He does not ask you to carry this year in your own ability. His strength is steady, patient, and ever-present. Even when you feel weak, He remains constant lifting what you cannot lift, holding what you cannot hold. His strength fills the spaces where yours falls short, reminding you that dependence on Him is not a burden but a blessing. When your heart trembles or your hands grow weary, His strength becomes your shelter, your support, and your quiet confidence. In His presence, weakness is not failure, it is an invitation for His power to rest upon you.

Prayer

Father, be my strength today. Fill the places that feel empty and renew the areas that feel weak. Thank You for being my steady support. When my courage wavers, remind me that You go before me. When I feel overwhelmed, let Your presence calm every anxious thought. Teach me to lean into Your strength instead of my own and help me trust that You are working even in the moments I cannot see. Wrap my heart in Your peace, steady my steps, and carry me with the quiet confidence that You are with me, guiding me through every season. Amen.

Blessing Declaration

God strengthens me daily. I walk in quiet, steady strength.

Personal Declaration (**Write Below**)

Today, I lean on God's strength in the area of

____

____

____

DAY 5

A Whisper of Courage

Be strong and of a good courage, fear not, nor be afraid of them: for the Lord thy God, he it is that doth go with thee; he will not fail thee, nor forsake thee.

Deuteronomy 31:6

Courage does not always roar. Sometimes it looks like soft bravery showing up to life even when you feel unsure, choosing faith when fear feels easier, or taking one small step when a giant leap seems impossible. Courage is often quiet and hidden, formed in the unseen places of the heart where God whispers strength into your spirit. It's found in the moments when you rise after falling, when you pray even though you feel weary, and when you hold onto hope despite not seeing the full picture. This gentle kind of courage is precious to God, for it reflects a heart that is willing to trust Him in the middle of uncertainty.

> *Joshua 1:9*
>
> *Have not I commanded thee? Be strong and of a good courage; be not afraid, neither be thou dismayed: for the Lord thy God is with thee whithersoever thou goes.*

God walks beside you. His presence gives you the courage to face the unknowns of this year. You are not doing this alone. **Deuteronomy 31:8** *And the Lord, he it is that does go before thee; he will be with thee, he will not fail thee, neither forsake thee: fear not, neither be dismayed.* Courage grows when you remember who goes with you. He steadies your trembling heart, strengthens your wavering steps, and surrounds you with a peace that anchors your soul. Every challenge becomes lighter when carried with Him. Every fear loses its voice when His truth speaks louder. As you move forward, let His companionship be your confidence. The God who called you is the same God who equips you, sustains you, and lovingly leads you into every new season.

Prayer

Lord, fill my heart with quiet courage today. Remove fear and replace it with confidence in Your presence. When my spirit feels hesitant, whisper reminders of Your faithfulness. When my steps feel uncertain, steady me with the strength only You can give. Teach me to trust Your leading even when the path is unclear and help me surrender every anxious thought into Your hands. Let Your peace rest over my mind, Your strength rise within my spirit, and Your love surround me like a shield. May I walk through this day with a boldness that comes not from myself, but from knowing that You are with me, guiding me, empowering me, and covering me in every season. Amen.

Blessing Declaration

I am courageous because God goes before me, walks beside me, and strengthens me from within. I face this year with bold faith, steady peace, and a heart anchored in His presence.

Personal Declaration (Write Below)

Today, I choose courage by taking this step:

____

____

____

DAY 6

A Whisper of Guidance

And the Lord shall guide thee continually, and satisfy thy soul in drought, and make fat thy bones: and thou shalt be like a watered garden, and like a spring of water, whose waters fail not.

Isaiah 58:11

God's guidance is gentle. It doesn't rush you it leads you. He guides you step by step, moment by moment, whisper by whisper. Even when you can't see the full picture, He illuminates the next step. His leading is never forceful or demanding; it is patient, kind, and full of wisdom. God knows exactly how to speak to your heart and how to steady you when uncertainty tries to cloud your vision. He walks with you through every choice, every pathway, and every season, quietly inviting you to lean into His direction and trust the soft impressions He places upon your spirit. Nothing about His guidance is careless, every nudge, every pause, every open- or closed-door forms part of His loving plan for your life.

> *Psalm 32:8*
>
> *I will instruct thee and teach thee in the way which thou shalt go: I will guide thee with mine eye.*

This year, trust His leading. Surrender your plans into His hands. He knows the way, He sees ahead, and He lovingly directs your path. **Proverbs 3:5-6** *Trust in the Lord with all thine heart; and lean not unto thine own understanding. In all thy ways acknowledge him, and he shall direct thy paths.* Even when the road bends unexpectedly or you face moments that feel unfamiliar, His presence stays constant. He prepares places you haven't reached yet and clears obstacles you'll never even see. When you release control and yield to His timing, you allow Him to lead you into blessings that your own strength could never reach. God is not only guiding you He is guarding you, shaping you, and positioning you for every purpose He has ordained. You can walk forward with peace, knowing your steps are held securely within His perfect wisdom.

Prayer

Father, guide me today. Make my steps clear and my spirit sensitive to Your direction. Help me to recognize Your voice above every distraction and quiet every thought that leads me away from Your peace. Teach me to trust the pauses just as much as the open doors, knowing that Your timing is perfect and Your plans are good. When I feel unsure, remind me that You go before me, preparing the way. When I feel hesitant, steady my heart with Your reassurance. Lead me with Your wisdom, surround me with Your presence, and shape my desires so they align with Your will. Walk with me through every choice I face today and let Your gentle hand be the compass that guides my steps. Amen.

Blessing Declaration

God guides my every step. His wisdom goes before me, His peace walks beside me, and His presence lights the path ahead. I trust His direction, surrender my plans to His will, and walk forward with confidence, knowing that He is leading me into purpose and peace.

Personal Declaration (**Write Below**)

Today, I will follow God's guidance in

____

____

____

DAY 7

A Whisper of Joy

Then he said unto them, Go your way, eat the fat, and drink the sweet, and send portions unto them for whom nothing is prepared: for this day is holy unto our Lord: neither be ye sorry; **for the joy of the Lord is your strength.**

Nehemiah 8:10

Joy is a gift God places deep within steady, gentle, and resilient. It's not dependent on circumstances, nor does it fade when life becomes challenging. This joy is rooted in the unchanging truth of who God is present, faithful, and working in ways you cannot yet see. It rises quietly in the soul, reminding you that even in the midst of uncertainty, there is a reason to hope. God's joy whispers strength into weary places and breathes light into the corners of your heart that feel dim. It is a joy that carries you, lifts you, and sustains you far beyond what your own strength could ever accomplish.

Philippians 4:4

Rejoice in the Lord always: and again I say, Rejoice.

Let joy be your companion this year. **Habakkuk 3:18** *Yet I will rejoice in the Lord, I will joy in the God of my salvation.* Let it rise in the morning and sustain you through the day, anchoring your heart in God's goodness. Let it soften your worries and brighten your path when things feel unclear. Joy renews you, strengthens you, and reminds you that you are held by a faithful God who walks with you in every season. It is the gentle reminder that God is still working, still shaping, still unfolding beauty from places that once felt heavy. When you choose joy even

quietly, even imperfectly you choose to align your heart with God's presence, allowing His light to shine through your life in ways you may never fully comprehend.

Prayer

Lord, fill my heart with Your joy today. Let it rise within me like a steady light that no circumstance can dim. Lift every heaviness that tries to settle over my spirit and replace it with the sweetness of Your presence. Teach me to rejoice not only in the moments that feel easy, but also in the places where I am still waiting, trusting, and learning to surrender. Let Your joy strengthen me when I feel weary and remind me that I am never walking through life alone. Surround me with the quiet assurance that You are working behind the scenes, weaving goodness into every part of my story. May Your joy overflow from my heart into my words, my actions, and every space I enter today. Let it be a reflection of Your love, shining through me with grace and gentleness. Amen.

Blessing Declaration

The joy of the Lord fills my heart and strengthens my every step. His joy lights my path, steadies my spirit, and flows through my life with peace and confidence.

Personal Declaration (**Write Below**)

Today, I choose joy by focusing on

____

____

____

Blessings for Purpose

This week invites you to lean into the quiet call of purpose God's unique plan unfolding in your life day by day. Purpose doesn't rush, and it rarely arrives all at once. It grows through clarity, wisdom, courage, and the gentle leading of the Holy Spirit. As you walk through these seven days, may God awaken new ideas, open new doors, and strengthen your confidence in the path He has prepared for you. Let His whisper guide you into deeper purpose, steady direction, and renewed vision for your life.

DAY 8

A Whisper of Clarity

Thy word is a lamp unto my feet, and a light unto my path.

Psalm 119:105

Clarity rarely arrives all at once. God often reveals purpose step by step, the way a lamp lights only the next part of the path. This gentle leading protects you from being overwhelmed and teaches you to lean on His presence rather than your own understanding. Even when the way ahead feels dim, His light is enough for the moment you're in, reminding you that He is guiding you with care and intention.

If you feel uncertain about where God is taking you, be comforted: **Jeremiah 29:11** *For I know the thoughts that I think toward you, saith the Lord, thoughts of peace, and not of evil, to give you an expected end.* He knows the way, the timing, and what your heart is ready to carry. Trust the small lights He gives moments of insight, peaceful nudges, quiet confirmations. These gentle reminders are His way of assuring you that you are moving in the right direction, held securely in His wisdom and love.

He is not hiding your purpose He is guiding you into it. With every step you take, He is shaping your understanding, strengthening your faith,

> *Isaiah 42:16*
>
> *And I will bring the blind by a way that they knew not; I will lead them in paths that they have not known: I will make darkness light before them, and crooked things straight. These things will I do unto them and not forsake them.*

and preparing your heart for what lies ahead. Even when clarity feels distant, trust that God is at work behind the scenes, aligning every detail and leading you toward the future He has lovingly designed for you.

Prayer

Lord, give me clarity today. Quiet every voice that brings confusion and let Your guidance rise gently within me. Light the step I need to take and steady my heart when I feel unsure. Help me recognize Your peace as confirmation and trust Your timing even when I cannot see the full picture. Align my thoughts with Your wisdom, my choices with Your will, and my spirit with Your calm. Lead me with the assurance that You are near, shaping my path with purpose and care. Amen.

Blessing Declaration

God lights my path and guides my steps with peace and purpose; I walk confidently in His wisdom today.

Personal Declaration (Write Below)

Today, I seek clarity from God in the area of

____

____

____

DAY 9

A Whisper of God-Given Ideas

But the Comforter, which is the Holy Ghost, whom the Father will send in my name, **he shall teach you all things**, and bring all things to your remembrance, whatsoever I have said unto you.

John 14:26

God speaks creativity into your spirit. He plants ideas, solutions, and visions that reflect His wisdom and beauty. The whisper you feel, the gentle stirring, the inspiration that won't leave is often His voice guiding you toward purpose. These ideas are not random thoughts; they are seeds placed intentionally by God, to grow in the right season and bring life, direction, and impact.

This year, expect God to breathe new ideas into you. Write them down. Pray over them. Habakkuk 2:2-3 *And the Lord answered me, and said, write the vision, and make it plain upon tables, that he may run that read it. For the vision is yet for an appointed time, but at the end it shall speak, and not lie: though it tarry, wait for it; because it will surely come, it will not tarry.* Let Him show you how they fit into your calling and the season you are in. What God inspires, He also empowers, providing the clarity, courage, and resources needed as you take one faithful step at a time.

> *Exodus 35:31-32*
>
> *And he hath filled him with the spirit of God, in wisdom, in understanding, and in knowledge, and in all manner of workmanship; And to devise curious works, to work in gold, and in silver, and in brass.*

Prayer

Father, thank You for the ideas You place within my heart. Help me to recognize what comes from You and to steward if with wisdom and faith. Quiet every doubt that tries to silence what You are stirring and give me courage to take the next small step You are asking of me. Guide my thoughts, strengthen my confidence, and let Your Spirit lead every idea toward the purpose You have prepared. Amen.

Blessing Declaration

God inspires my thoughts and empowers every idea He places within me.

Personal Declaration (Write Below)

Today, I will honor my God-given idea of _______ by taking one step toward it.

____

____

____

DAY 10

A Whisper of Open Doors

I know thy works: behold, I have set before thee an open door, and no man can shut it: for thou hast a little strength, and hast kept my word, and hast not denied my name.

Revelation 3:8

Every open door from God carries peace. You don't have to force it, beg for it, or manipulate your way through it. When God opens a door, it stays open not by your strength but by His authority. His peace acts as confirmation, gently assuring your heart that the path before you is aligned with His will and covered by His grace.

This year, trust Him for divine opportunities. Some doors may close, not because you are unworthy, but because He has something better prepared. **Isaiah 55:8-9** *For my thoughts are not your thoughts, neither are your ways my ways, saith the Lord. For as the heavens are higher than the earth, so are my ways higher than your ways, and my thoughts than your thoughts.* Let your heart stay soft and expectant, even in moments of disappointment or delay. God is faithful to open the right doors at the right time, leading you into places that protect your peace and align with His greater purpose for your life.

> *Psalm 127:1*
>
> *Except the Lord build the house, they labor in vain that build it: except the Lord keep the city, the watchman wake but in vain.*

Prayer

Lord, open the doors You have prepared for me and close the ones that are not meant for my life. Lead me into the places You bless. Give me discernment to recognize Your hand at work and peace to trust You when answers unfold slowly. Help me release fear, impatience, and doubt and replace them with confidence in Your timing. As You guide my steps, let my heart remain surrendered, trusting that every door You open will lead me closer to Your purpose and peace. Amen.

Blessing Declaration

God opens the right doors for me. I step into His opportunities with peace.

Personal Declaration (**Write Below**)

Today, I release closed doors and choose to trust God for new ones in

____

____

____

DAY 11

A Whisper of Divine Appointments

The steps of a good man are ordered by the Lord: and he delighted in his way.

Psalm 37:23

God is intentional with your connections. He weaves people into your life with care and purpose some to encourage your heart when you feel weary, some to teach you lessons that shape your growth, some to walk beside you through seasons of transition, and some to help lift you into the next chapter He has prepared. Each relationship carries meaning, even if its role is brief. God uses these connections to refine you, strengthen you, and remind you that you were never meant to journey alone.

Psalm 25:4-5

Shew me thy ways, O Lord; teach me thy paths. Lead me in thy truth and teach me: for thou art the God of my salvation; on thee do I wait all the day.

Nothing is random when God orders your steps. The conversation that lingers in your mind, the encounter you didn't plan for, the opportunity that seemed unexpected He is present in every detail. Even what feels ordinary or coincidental is often divinely arranged. Trust that God knows exactly who you need and when you need them. As you remain open and prayerful, He will continue to align the right people at the right time, guiding your path with wisdom, grace, and purpose.

Prayer

Father, order my steps today. Align my life with the people and places You have chosen for my purpose. Lead me into conversations that bring encouragement, connections that bring growth, and opportunities that reflect Your will. Remove distractions and misaligned paths and give me discernment to recognize what comes from You. Help me walk with humility, wisdom, and openness, trusting that every step You arrange is guided by Your love and perfect timing. Amen.

Blessing Declaration

God orders my steps. I am aligned with divine appointments and purposeful connections.

Personal Declaration (Write Below)

Today, I open my heart to divine connections in the area of

____

____

____

DAY 12

A Whisper of Renewed Purpose

For we are his workmanship, created in Christ Jesus unto good works, which God hath before ordained that we should walk in them.

Ephesians 2:10

Purpose is not something you create, it is something you discover. God formed you with intention, gifting, and spiritual design, weaving purpose into your life long before you were aware of it. When life feels confusing or heavy, He gently restores what has been buried under stress, fear, or disappointment reminding your heart that nothing He placed within you was ever lost.

This year, allow Him to breathe new life into your purpose. Let Him refresh your confidence and remind you who you are in Him: chosen, gifted, prepared. **Psalm 138:8**

> **Jeremiah 1.5**
>
> *Before I formed thee in the belly I knew thee; and before thou came forth out of the womb, I sanctified thee, and I ordained thee a prophet unto the nations.*

The Lord will perfect that which concern me: thy mercy, O Lord, endures for ever: forsake not the works of thine own hands. As you draw closer to Him, He renews your clarity and strengthens your trust, helping you see yourself through His loving and purposeful design.

Your purpose has never left. God is simply awakening it again stirring what has been quiet, reviving what felt distant, and guiding you gently back into the calling He has always held for you.

Prayer

Lord, renew my sense of purpose. Help me remember who I am in You and what You created me to do. Restore my confidence when doubt tries to cloud my vision and guide my steps with clarity and peace. Remind me that my calling is held securely in Your hands and that You are faithfully leading me forward. Amen.

Blessing Declaration

My purpose is alive in God. He renews my calling day by day.

Personal Declaration (**Write Below**)

Today, I choose to walk in renewed purpose by focusing on

____

____

____

DAY 13

A Whisper of Wisdom

If any of you lack wisdom, let him ask of God, that giveth to all men liberally, and upbraideth not; and it shall be given him.

James 1:5

Wisdom is one of God's softest blessings. It doesn't always come through dramatic revelation sometimes it comes as a quiet knowing, a gentle redirection, or a peaceful "yes" or "no" in your spirit. It settles calmly within your heart, bringing assurance rather than urgency, and guiding you with a steadiness that invites trust instead of fear. God's wisdom often whispers, patiently leading you toward what is best rather than what is simply immediate.

> *James 3:17*
>
> *But the wisdom that is from above is first pure, then peaceable, gentle, and easy to be intreated, full of mercy and good fruits, without partiality, and without hypocrisy.*

When you seek God's wisdom, He responds not reluctantly, but generously. **Proverbs 2:6** *For the Lord giveth wisdom: out of his mouth cometh knowledge and understanding.* He longs to guide you with clarity, insight, and truth, meeting your question with understanding and care. This year, let His wisdom shape your decisions, conversations, and direction, allowing His peace to confirm each step you take. As you lean into His guidance, you'll find that His wisdom gently aligns your path with His purpose.

Prayer

Lord, I come to You in need of Your wisdom. Guide my thoughts, shape my decisions, and quiet every voice that brings confusion. Help me to pause and seek You before I act, trusting that You will lead me with clarity and peace. Teach me to listen closely to Your gentle promptings and to walk in understanding rather than haste. Let Your wisdom guard my heart and direct my steps as I move through this day. Amen.

Blessing Declaration

God fills me with His wisdom. I walk in clarity, discernment, and peace as He directs my steps.

Personal Declaration (Write Below)

Today, I choose to seek God's wisdom in ______. I will pause, listen, and trust His guidance as I move forward.

____

____

____

DAY 14

A Whisper of Blessing Over Your Work

Commit thy works unto the Lord, and thy thoughts shall be established.

Proverbs 16:3

Your work whatever form it takes is sacred when placed in God's hands. He blesses the work that is surrendered to Him, not only the visible outcomes but the quiet faithfulness behind each effort. He brings fruit to the labor you offer, peace to the tasks you complete, and grace to the assignments that stretch or challenge you. Even the work that feels ordinary or unseen matters to God, because He sees the heart and intention behind every step you take.

> *Isaiah 48:17*
>
> *Thus saith the Lord, thy Redeemer, the Holy One of Israel; I am the Lord thy God which teach thee to profit, which leadeth thee by the way that thou should go.*

This year, entrust your work to Him. **Psalm 37:5** *Commit thy way unto the Lord; trust also in him; and he shall bring it to pass.* Let Him bless your ideas, strengthen your diligence, and bring success according to His purpose not pressure. You were never meant to carry your workload alone. God works with you, through you, and ahead of you, ordering details you cannot see and preparing outcomes you have not yet imagined. As you commit your work to Him, He will steady your pace, guard your peace, and guide your efforts with wisdom and favor.

Prayer

Lord, I commit my work to You. Bless the efforts of my hands and establish the plans that align with Your will. Give me clarity when I feel unsure, perseverance when I feel weary, and peace when responsibilities feel heavy. Help me to work with integrity, purpose, and trust, knowing that You are present in every task I take on. I place my work in Your care and rest in the assurance that You are guiding it for good. Amen.

Blessing Declaration

God blesses the work of my hands. My efforts prosper under His guidance.

Personal Declaration (Write Below)

Today, I dedicate my work to God by surrendering

____

____

____

Blessings for Healing & Wholeness

This week invites you to rest in God's restoring presence. Healing and wholeness often unfold quietly through patience, surrender, and the gentle touch of God's love. As you move through these days, may God bring renewal to every area of your life, mending what feels broken, strengthening what feels weak, and reminding you that He is near, attentive, and deeply committed to your restoration.

DAY 15

A Whisper of Emotional Healing

He heals the broken in heart and binds up their wounds.

Psalm 147:3

Emotional healing often begins quietly through tears, through honesty, through a soft openness to God's presence. It starts when you allow yourself to feel what you've been holding back and invite God into those tender places. There is no timeline for healing, no expectation to "move on" before you're ready. God walks with you patiently, never rushing the process, gently meeting you where your heart feels fragile and exposed.

> **Psalm 34:18**
>
> The Lord is nigh unto them that are of a broken heart; and saves such as be of a contrite spirit.

He does not rush your restoration. He sits with you in the ache, listens to the prayers you struggle to put into words, and gathers every sorrow you carry. In His presence, your pain is not dismissed or minimized it is seen and held with compassion. Healing is not the absence of pain; it is the steady awareness that God is near, sustaining you even in the middle of it.

Little by little, He is binding up every wound. **Psalm 34:19** *Many are the afflictions of the righteous: but the Lord delivered him out of them all.* Each moment of surrender, each quiet prayer, each breath taken in His presence becomes part of the healing work He is doing within you. Though progress may feel slow, restoration is unfolding with care and intention. God is faithful to heal what has been broken, bringing wholeness in His perfect time and gentle way.

Prayer

Lord, touch the places in my heart that need healing. Restore what has been broken and breathe peace into my emotions. Sit with me in the moments that feel heavy and remind me that I am not alone in my pain. Help me release what I have been carrying and trust You with every tender place within me. Cover my heart with Your love, steady my spirit with Your presence, and lead me gently toward wholeness and rest. Amen.

Blessing Declaration

God heals my heart gently. Emotional restoration flows through my life.

Personal Declaration (Write Below)

Today, I open my heart to healing in the area of

____

____

____

DAY 16

A Whisper of Physical Healing

Who forgives all thine iniquities; **who healeth all thy diseases.**

Psalm 103:3

God cares deeply about your physical body. He sees every ache, every weakness, every diagnosis, and every moment you feel tired or discouraged. Nothing you experience goes unnoticed by Him. Whether your healing comes instantly, gradually, or through the wisdom and care of the doctors, His presence remains close, steady, and attentive. He strengthens you not only in the outcome but in the waiting, surrounding you with hope, patience, and quiet reassurance that you are held in His care.

Healing is not always dramatic; sometimes it unfolds slowly and quietly. It may look like the steady renewal of energy, small improvement over time, or moments of unexpected relief that remind you God is near. Trust that even when you cannot see immediate change, God is working beneath the surface. His healing is both a promise and a process, one marked by compassion, faithfulness, and perfect timing. **Isaiah 57:18-19**

Isaiah 53:4-5

Surely he hath borne our griefs and carried our sorrows: yet we did esteem him stricken, smitten of God, and afflicted.

But he was wounded for our transgressions, he was bruised for our iniquities: the chastisement of our peace was upon him; **and with his stripes we are healed.**

I have seen his ways and will heal him: I will lead him also and restore comforts unto him and to his mourners. I create the fruit of the lips; Peace, peace to him that is far off, and to him that is near, saith the Lord; and I will heal him. Each step forward, no matter how small, is part of the restoration He is gently bringing to your life.

Prayer

Lord, You are my healer. Strengthen my body, restore my health, and let Your healing power flow through me. Touch every place that feels weak, weary, or in need of renewal, and bring peace where there has been discomfort or concern. Help me trust You through each step of the healing process, whether it comes quickly or unfolds over time. Surround me with Your presence, steady my heart with hope, and renew my strength day by day as I rest in Your loving care. Amen.

Blessing Declaration

God is my healer. His strength renews my body day by day.

Personal Declaration (**Write Below**)

Today, I speak healing over my body in the area of

____

____

____

DAY 17

A Whisper of Spiritual Renewal

Create in me a clean heart, O God; and renew a right spirit within me.

Psalm 51:10

Spiritual renewal is one of God's tender gifts. He refreshes your spirit when you feel dry, strengthens you when you feel distant, and restores your desire for His presence when it has grown faint. Renewal that God has not moved away from you even in seasons when you feel weary or disconnected. His Spirit patiently revives what feels worn, breathing new life into your faith and gently drawing you back into communion with Him.

> **Psalm 23:3**
>
> *He restoreth my soul: he leadeth me in the paths of righteousness for his name's sake.*

There is no shame in needing renewal. God continually draws you closer, inviting you into moments of stillness where your soul can breathe again and your heart can rest. He is not disappointed by your need He welcomes it. **Matthew 11:28** *Come unto me, all ye that labour and are heavy laden, and I will give you rest.* In His presence, exhaustion gives way to peace and heaviness begins to lift. Let him refill you where you feel empty. Let Him restore joy to your walk with Him, not as something forced, but as something naturally renewed through His nearness.

He delights in renewing you. With great compassion, God restores what feels tired and rekindles what has grown quiet within you. **Isaiah 40:31** *But they that wait upon the Lord shall renew their strength; they shall mount up with wings as eagles; they shall run and not be weary; and they shall walk,* *and not faint.* Each moment you turn toward Him becomes an opportunity for renewal, reminding you that His grace is ongoing and His mercy is always at work, gently shaping and refreshing your spirit day by day.

Prayer

Father, renew my spirit today. Draw me closer to You and awaken a fresh desire for Your presence. Refresh my heart where it feels weary and restore my joy where it has grown quiet. Help me slow down enough to recognize Your nearness and rest in the peace You freely give. Fill me again with Your strength, Your love, and Your gentle guidance, and let my spirit be renewed as I walk with You through this day. Amen.

Blessing Declaration

God renews my spirit. My heart grows steady, restored, and refreshed in Him.

Personal Declaration (**Write Below**)

Today, I welcome spiritual renewal by committing to

____

____

____

DAY 18

A Whisper of Protection

But the Lord is faithful, who shall stablish you, and keep you from evil.

2 Thessalonians 3:3

You are covered. Even when life feels uncertain, God places His protection around you, over your home, your mind, your path and your purpose. His protection is not always visible, but it is always present, steady and faithful. In moments when you feel vulnerable or unsure, His covering remains constant, surrounding you with a peace that reassures your heart that you are not exposed or forgotten.

> *Psalm 121:7-8*
>
> *The Lord shall preserve thee from all evil: he shall preserve thy soul. The Lord shall preserve thy going out and thy coming in from this time forth, and even for evermore.*

God goes before you, stands beside you, and guards what concerns you. **Deuteronomy 31:8** *And the Lord, he it is that doth go before thee; he will be with thee, he will not fail thee, neither forsake thee: fear not, neither be dismayed.* He watches over the details you cannot foresee and shields you from what you may never know was coming. **Psalm 34:7** *The angel of the Lord encamped round about them that fear him, and delivered them.* The dangers you never saw, the storms that never formed, the attacks that never reached you, these are quiet testimonies of His loving care. Even when you are unaware, God is actively working to protect, preserve, and guide you.

Rest today in the assurance that God is watching over you. You do not have to remain alert or anxious to stay safe, He is already attentive. As you place your trust in Him, allow your spirit to settle, knowing that His faithful covering surrounds you today and every day.

Prayer

Lord, thank You for Your protection. Surround my life, my mind, and my home with Your covering. Guard my thoughts with Your peace, shield my heart from fear, and place Your presence over every space I enter. Keep me safe in Your hands as I go about this day, watching over what concerns me and what I cannot see. Help me rest in the assurance that You are near, attentive, and faithful to protect me in every moment.

Amen

Blessing Declaration

God protects me. His covering surrounds every part of my life.

Personal Declaration (**Write Below**)

Today, I trust God's protection over

____

____

____

DAY 19

A Whisper of Freedom from Fear

For God has not given us a spirit of fear, but of power, and of love, and of a sound mind.

2 Timothy 1:7

Fear is loud, but God's reassurance is louder. His love settles the anxieties that rise in your heart and reminds you of the power He placed within you. Fear may knock, but it does not have to stay, You are not required to entertain every fearful thought or carry every worry that tries to attach itself to you. God's presence brings a deeper voice one that speaks peace safety, and truth over the noise. When fear begins to rise, His love gently quiets your spirit and anchors you in what is unchanging.

> **Isaiah 41:10**
>
> Fear thou not; for I am with thee: be not dismayed; for I am thy God: I will strengthen thee; yea, I will help thee; yea, I will uphold thee with the right hand of my righteousness.

This year, let God replace fear with truth. **John 8:32** *And ye shall know the truth, and the truth shall make you free.* Let Him steady your mind when thoughts feel scattered and strengthen your confidence when uncertainty tries to weaken you. God continually reminds you that you are never facing life alone He walks with you, stands besides you and goes before you. Courage grows not from the absence of fear, but from choosing to remain close to God's presence. As you hold onto Him, fear loses its grip and faith finds room to rise.

Here Are Some Ways To Release Fear

- **Name it in prayer**. Speak your fear honestly to God instead of carrying it silently.
- **Replace it with truth**. When fear speaks, counter it with God's promises and reminders of His faithfulness.
- **Release control daily**. Surrender what you cannot fix and trust God with the outcome.
- **Stay close to God's presence**. Fear weakens when you remain anchored in prayer, scripture, and quiet moments with Him.

Prayer

Lord, remove fear from my heart. Fill me with Your power, Your love, and a sound, steady mind. Quiet every anxious thought that tries to rise within me and replace it with Your truth and peace. Help me trust You more deeply, especially in moments when uncertainty feel close. Teach me to walk forward with confidence rooted in Your presence, not my circumstances. Let Your peace guard my heart, steady my steps, and remind me that I am never alone. I place my fears in Your hands and choose faith over fear today. Amen.

Blessing Declaration

I am free from fear. God fills me with strength, love, and a sound mind.

Personal Declaration (Write Below)

Today, I release fear about ______________ and choose to trust God instead.

____

____

____

DAY 20

A Whisper of Strength in Trials

And he said unto me, My grace is sufficient for thee: for my strength is made perfect in weakness. Most gladly therefore will I rather glory in my infirmities, that the power of Christ may rest upon me.

2 Corinthians 12:9

Trials do not mean God has abandoned you. They are not signs of His absence but often places where His nearness becomes most personal. In seasons of difficulty, God's strength does not arrive with noise of force it comes quietly, steadying your heart when everything feels unsteady. When your own ability runs out and you feel stretched beyond what you can manage, His grace steps in with compassion. It holds you when you feel weak, comforts you when you feel overwhelmed, and carries you through moments you could not endure on your own.

> **Psalm 34:19**
>
> *Many are the afflictions of the righteous: but the Lord delivered him out of them all.*

God does not expect you to carry every burden. **Psalm 55:22** *Cast thy burden upon the Lord, and he shall sustain thee: he shall never suffer the righteous to be moved.* He knows your limits, sees your struggle, and understands the weight you are carrying both seen and unseen. He strengthens you in the very place where you feel weakest, reminding you that dependence on Him is not failure, but faith. His grace meets you right where you are, supplying what you lack and restoring what feels depleted. Even when the trial remains, His strength becomes enough more than enough to sustain you day by day.

Ways to Be Strengthened During Trials

- **Lean into God's grace daily**. Acknowledge your weakness and invite His strength into it.
- **Release what you cannot control**. Strength grows when you surrender the outcome to God.
- **Take one step at a time**. You don't need all the answers just the grace for today.
- **Speak truth over your situation**. Remind yourself that God is working even when you cannot see it.

Prayer

Lord, be my strength in every trial. Let Your grace lift what I cannot carry and renew my spirit when I feel weary. When my heart feels heavy and my energy feels low, remind me that I do not walk through this season alone. Steady me when my faith feels fragile and help me rest in the sufficiency of Your grace. Teach me to lean on You moment by moment, trusting that You are working even when the way feels difficult. Fill me with quiet endurance, lasting hope, and the assurance that Your strength is sustaining me through every step. Amen.

Blessing Declaration

God's strength sustains me. His grace meets me where I am

Personal Declaration (**Write Below**)

Today, I will lean on God's strength in the challenge of

____

____

____

DAY 21

A Whisper of Hope Reignited

Now the God of hope fill you with all joy and peace in believing, that ye may abound in hope, through the power of the Holy Ghost.

Romans 15:13

Hope is a gentle flame. Sometimes it burns brightly; other times it flickers softly, barely noticeable beneath the weight of disappointment or waiting. God knows when your hope feels fragile. He sees the moments when you've grown tired of believing and weary of expecting. With tender care, He leans close and breathes on the embers, reigniting what life tried to dim. Even when hope feels faint, it is never extinguished in His hands. God specializes in reviving what looks small, weak, or nearly gone.

Hebrews 6:19

Which hope we have as an anchor of the soul, both sure and stedfast, and which entered into that within the veil;

Hope reminds you that your story is not finished. God is still working, still moving, still weaving beauty into places that once felt broken or delayed. What feels incomplete now is still being shaped by His faithfulness. Let hope rise again not loudly or all at once, but quietly, like light returning at dawn. As the sun rises slowly and steadily, so does hope, reminding you that new mercies are unfolding and that God is bringing life where you least expect it.

Ways to Reignite Hope

- **Remember God's past faithfulness.** Reflect on moments when He carried you through before, what He has done once, He can do again.
- **Anchor your heart in truth.** When circumstances feel heavy, return to God's promises and let His Word speak louder than discouragement.
- **Allow hope to grow quietly.** You don't need to feel strong to be hopeful sometimes hope begins with simply choosing to trust God one day at a time.

Prayer

God of hope, breathe on my heart today. Restore joy where it has faded, renew peace where it has been shaken, and let hope rise again within me. When my spirit feels weary or discouraged, remind me that You are still working and that my story is still unfolding in Your hands. Help me trust You even when I cannot see what lies ahead and anchor my heart in Your faithfulness. Fill me with quiet expectation, steady assurance, and the gentle confidence that brighter days are coming through You. Amen.

Blessing Declaration

Hope is rising within me. God fills me with joy, peace, and renewed expectation.

Personal Declaration (**Write Below**)

Today, I choose to hope again in the area of

____

____

____

Blessings for Abundance & Growth

This final week invites you to step forward with truth and expectation. As God continues His work within you, may He bring growth where seeds have been planted and abundance where you have faithfully waited. Abundance does not always arrive loudly it often unfolds through peace, provision, gratitude, and steady growth. As you walk through these final days, may your heart remain open to all that God is gently bringing forth, and may you step into the year ahead with confidence, gratitude, and renewed faith.

DAY 22

A Whisper of Provision

But my God shall supply all your need according to His riches in glory by Christ Jesus.

Philippians 4:19

God's provision is tender and timely. He sees every need spoken and unspoken and nothing about your life escapes His attention. He understands what your heart requires and what your days demand, even when you struggle to put those needs into words. His provision may not always arrive in the form you expect, but it always comes with intention, wisdom, and peace. God provides not only what you need to survive, but what you need to be sustained strength for today, grace for the moment, and reassurance for your heart.

As you move through this year, trust His faithfulness. What you need will meet you at the moment you need it, not a moment too early or too late. **Isaiah 45:2** *I will go before thee, and make the crooked places straight: I will break in pieces the gates of brass, and cut in sunder the bars of iron:* God has already gone ahead of you, preparing provision for

> *Matthew 6:31-33*
>
> *Therefore take no thought, saying, What shall we eat? or, What shall we drink? or, Wherewithal shall we be clothed? (For after all these things do the Gentiles seek:) for your heavenly Father knows that you have need of all these things. But seek ye first the kingdom of God, and his righteousness; and all these things shall be added unto you.*

every season you will face. Even in times of waiting, He is working quietly behind the scenes, aligning resources, opportunities, and support in ways you may not yet see. Each day carries its own portion of grace, and God is faithful to supply enough for today while gently leading you into tomorrow.

Prayer

Lord, I trust You as my provider. Meet my needs in Your perfect timing and help me rest in Your care. When uncertainty tries to rise, steady my heart with the assurance of Your faithfulness. Teach me to rely on You daily, releasing worry and embracing trust. Thank You for providing not only what I need, but the peace that comes from knowing You are always watching over me. Amen

Blessing Declaration

God supplies all my needs. His provision flows into my life with grace and peace.

Personal Declaration (**Write Below**)

Today, I trust God's provision concerning

____

____

____

DAY 23

A Whisper of Unexpected Blessings

Surely goodness and mercy shall follow me all the days of my life: and I will dwell in the house of the Lord for ever.

Psalm 23:6

God loves to surprise you with His goodness. Sometimes blessings unfold slowly, like seeds growing beneath the surface, and other times they arrive suddenly through answered prayers, a lifted burden, an unexpected opportunity, or a moment of peace you didn't see coming. God delights in meeting you in ways that remind you He is attentive to every detail of your life. Even when you feel unseen or uncertain, His goodness is already at work, quietly preparing moments that will restore your hope and renew your strength.

Psalm 31:19

Oh how great is thy goodness, which thou hast laid up for them that fear thee; which thou hast wrought for them that trust in thee before the sons of men!

Open your heart to the joy of unexpected blessings. God is not limited by circumstance, timing, or what feels possible to you. **Ephesians 3:20** *Now unto him that is able to do exceeding abundantly above all that we ask or think, according to the power that worketh in us.* He is creative, generous, and deeply personal in the way He cares for you. His goodness follows you, surrounds you, and gently overtakes you in the moments you need it most often when your heart is weary or your expectations are low. As you remain open and trusting, you may begin to notice His blessing not only in big moments, but also in small, scared reminders of His love.

Prayer

Lord, I welcome Your unexpected blessings. Open my eyes to recognize Your goodness when it appears in quiet and surprising ways. Help me remain hopeful, trusting that You are working beyond what I can see or imagine. Let Your grace meet me in the ordinary moments and your joy rise in the places I least expect. Thank You for Your faithfulness, Your generosity, and the gentle ways You remind me that I am deeply cared for. Amen.

Blessing Declaration

God's goodness follows me. I receive unexpected blessings with gratitude.

Personal Declaration **(Write Below)**

Today, I open my heart to unexpected blessings in

____

____

____

DAY 24

A Whisper of Peace in the Waiting

Rest in the Lord and wait patiently for him: fret not thyself because of him who prosper in his way, because of the man who brings wicked devices to pass.

Psalm 37:7

Waiting is one of the softest tests of faith. It stretches your trust, quiets your spirit, and deepens your dependence on God in ways that constant movement never could. Waiting invites you to release control and lean into God's presence rather than rushing ahead for answers. Though it may feel uncomfortable or uncertain, waiting creates space for your faith to mature, your heart to be refined, and your trust to grow stronger. Waiting is not wasted time it is shaping time, where God works patiently within you.

> *Psalm 27:14*
>
> *Wait on the Lord:*
> *be of good courage,*
> *and he shall*
> *strengthen thine*
> *heart: wait, I say,*
> *on the Lord.*

God works behind the scenes while you wait. **Psalm 46:10** *Be still and know that I am God:* He aligns details you cannot see, prepares hearts you have not yet met, rearranges circumstances for your good, and strengthens you for what is coming next. Even when nothing appears to be changing, God is active and attentive. You can rest in knowing that delays are often divine protection or divine preparation, guarding you from what is not ready and positioning you for what will be. What feels like waiting is often God's quiet work unfolding with care and purpose.

Prayer

Lord, teach me to wait with peace. Let patience settle gently in my spirit as I trust Your perfect timing. When waiting feels difficult, help me rest in the assurance that You are working on my behalf. Quiet my anxious thoughts, strengthen my faith, and help me surrender control into Your hands. I choose to trust that Your timing is wise, loving, and always for my good. Amen.

Blessing Declaration

God gives me peace while I wait. My spirit rests in His timing.

Personal Declaration (**Write Below**)

Today, I will wait with peace concerning

____

____

____

DAY 25

A Whisper of Blessing Over Relationships

And above all these things put on love, which is the bond of perfectness.

Colossians 3:14

Relationships are sacred places where God reveals His love and grace. He cares deeply about who surrounds you, who speaks into your life, and who walks beside you though each season. The people connected to your life have the power to influence your peace, your growth, and your faith. This year, may your relationships be marked by patience that listens, forgiveness that heals, clarity that brings understanding, and love that reflects God's heart. May each connection become a place where grace is exchanged and mutual growth is nurtured.

God is able to restore broken connections, strengthen healthy ones, and gently lead you away from relationships that no longer align with your purpose. **Joel 2:25** *And I will restore to you the years that the locust hath eaten, the cankerworm, and the caterpiller, and the palmerworm, my great army which I sent among you.* Nothing about your relational journey is overlooked by Him. He knows which relationships that shape you to remove what drains you and reinforce

Ecclesiastes 3:11

He hath made every thing beautiful in his time: also he hath set the world in their heart, so that no man can find out the work that God maketh from the beginning to the end.

what brings life, peace, and encouragement. As you follow His leading, He will surround you with connection that support the person He is calling you to become.

Prayer

Lord, bless my relationships. Bring harmony where there has been tension, healing where there has hurt, and love where there has been distance. Give me wisdom to nurture healthy connections and courage to release those that no longer serve Your purpose in my life. Help me love others with patience, humility, and grace, just as You have loved me. Lead me into relationships that reflect Your peace and strengthen my walk with You. Amen.

Blessing Declaration

God blesses my relationships. Love, harmony, healing, and into every connection You desire for my life. Amen.

Personal Declaration (**Write Below**)

Today, I speak blessing over my relationship with

____

____

____

DAY 26

A Whisper of Growth in Faith

But grow in grace, and in the knowledge of our Lord and Saviour Jesus Christ. To him be glory both now and for ever. Amen.

2 Peter 3:18

Growth often happens quietly. It's the deepening of trust, the softening of your heart, and the settling of your spirit as you learn to rest more fully in God. Faith grows not only in mountain-top moments, but in the ordinary, unseen choices you make each day to trust God when answers are unclear, to seek Him when life feels busy, and to follow His whisper even when it requires patience. These quiet moments of obedience and surrender slowly shape your faith, anchoring it deeper than emotional highs ever could.

> *Luke 16:10*
>
> *He that is faithful in that which is least is faithful also in much: and he that is unjust in the least is unjust also in much.*

This year, may your faith deepen through gentle consistency. Growth does not demand perfection, only willingness. Little by little, God strengthens your spiritual roots, teaching you to rely on Him with greater confidence and peace. **1 Thessalonians 5:24** *Faithful is he that calleth you, who also will do it.* As you continue to show up praying, listening, trusting He grows you into the person He has called you to be, steady and secure in His love. What feels small today is becoming something strong and lasting in His hands.

Ways to Grow in Faith

- **Stay consistent, not perfect**. Faith grows through regular, simple moments with God, prayer, reflection, and trust rather than occasional intensity.
- **Choose trust in uncertainty.** Each time you trust God without having all the answers, your faith stretches and strengthens.
- **Remain close to God's presence**. Growth happens naturally when you stay connected to Him, allowing His peace and truth to shape your heart daily.

Prayer

Lord, help my faith grow this year. Strengthen my trust when it feels fragile and deepen my desire to know You more. Teach me to remain faithful in small moments and patient in seasons of waiting. When doubt tries to rise, remind me of Your faithfulness, and when my spirit feels weary, renew my confidence in You. Root my faith deeply in Your truth and lead me forward with quiet assurance and peace. Amen.

Blessing Declaration

My faith grows daily. God nurtures my spirit with grace and truth.

Personal Declaration (**Write Below**)

Today, I will grow in faith by committing to

____

____

____

DAY 27

A Whisper of God's Faithfulness

It is of the Lord's mercies that we are not consumed, because his compassions fail not. They are new every morning: great is thy faithfulness.

Lamentations 3:22-23

Look back over your life and you will see it, God's faithfulness, woven through every season. Even in the moments you didn't understand, His hand was steady. Even when life changed, He remained constant. Scripture reminds us that **Hebrews 13:8** *Jesus Christ the same yesterday, and to day and for ever.* There were seasons when you questioned, waited, or felt unsure, yet God was quietly sustaining you. He carried you through what you could not carry alone, proving again and again that His faithfulness does not depend on circumstances, but on His unchanging nature.

> *Psalm 36:5*
>
> *Thy mercy, O Lord, is in the heavens; and thy faithfulness reaches unto the clouds.*

Let this year be marked by remembering His faithfulness. What He started, he will complete. What He promised, He will fulfill. What He spoke, He will bring to pass. **Philippians 1:6** *Being confident of this very thing, that he which hath begun a good work in you will perform it.* God does not abandon what He begins. His promises do not expire, and His word does not return void. As you remember His past faithfulness, your heart is strengthened to trust Him for what is still unfolding ahead.

Three Gentle Reminders of God's Faithfulness

1. *God has been faithful before and He will be faithful again.*
   Great is thy faithfulness. – Lamentations 3:23
2. **God finishes what He starts.** *The Lord will perfect that which concerneth me – Psalm 138:8*
3. **God remains faithful even when life feels uncertain.** *God is faithful. – 1 Corinthians 1:9*

Prayer

Lord, thank You for Your faithfulness. Thank You for every season You carried me through, every promise You kept, and every moment You remained near even when I could not see You clearly. Help me remember Your goodness when doubt tries to rise and anchor my heart in the truth that You never change. Teach me to trust You not only for what I have seen, but for what You are still working out in my life. I rest in the assurance that I am held by a faithful God whose mercy is new every morning. Amen.

Blessing Declaration

God is faithful in every season. His promises over my life stand firm.

Personal Declaration (**Write Below**)

Today, I will trust God's faithfulness in the area of

____

____

____

DAY 28

A Whisper of Gratitude

In everything give thanks: for this is the will of God in Christ Jesus concerning you.

1 Thessalonians 5:18

Gratitude softens the heart. It shifts your perspective from what is missing to what is present, from what hurts to what heals, from what feels delayed to what God is quietly developing. When gratitude takes root, it gently loosens the grip of discouragement and reminds you that God is still at work. Scripture tells us, *"In every thing give thanks"* (**1 Thessalonians 5:18**), not because every moment is easy, but because God's goodness can be found even in the midst of uncertainty. Gratitude helps you notice His nearness in places you may have overlooked.

Psalm 107:1

O give thanks unto the Lord, for he is good: for his mercy endured forever.

A grateful heart attracts peace. It opens your eyes to blessings you may have passed by too quickly and strengthens you though seasons when answers feel slow. **Philippians 4:6-7** *Be careful for nothing; but in every thing by prayer and supplication with thanksgiving let your requests be made known unto God.* Gratitude quiets anxious thoughts and invites God's peace to guard your heart. Today, let gratitude be your quiet offering to God not loud or forced, but sincere and steady trusting that He receives it with delight.

Ways to Show Gratitude from the Heart

- **Pause and acknowledge God daily**. Take a moment each day to thank Him for specific blessings, both big and small.
- **Give thanks before answers arrive.** Gratitude grows faith when you thank God even while you are still waiting.
- **Express gratitude through obedience and trust**. A thankful heart is shown not only in words, but in choosing to trust God with each step.

Prayer

Lord, cultivate a heart of gratitude within me. Help me recognize Your goodness in every moment, even when life feels ordinary or uncertain. Open my eyes to the blessings I've overlooked and soften my heart toward the gifts You place in my path each day. Teach me to give thanks not only for what You have done, but for who You are faithful, present, and good. Let gratitude become a rhythm in my life, drawing me closer to Your peace and deepening my trust in You. Amen.

Blessing Declaration

My heart overflows with gratitude. I see God's goodness all around me.

Personal Declaration (Write Below)

Today, I express gratitude for

____

DAY 29

A Whisper of Blessing Over Your Home

And my people shall dwell in a peaceable habitation, and in sure dwellings, and in quiet resting places.

Isaiah 32:18

Your home is more than a space, it's a sanctuary. It is a place where hearts rest, conversations unfold, and faith is quietly lived out day by day. God desires your home to be dwelling marked by peace, comfort, and protection a place where His presence is welcomed and felt. Scripture reminds us, " *My people shall dwell in a peaceable habitation, and in sure dwellings, and in quiet resting places"* (**Isaiah 32:18**). Whether your home is filled with activity or stillness, God longs to cover it with His peace and make it a refuge from the noise of the world.

> *Proverbs 3:33*
>
> *The curse of the Lord is in the house of the wicked: but he blessed the habitation of the just.*

Let this year bring a fresh covering over your home. May every room be filled with peace, every heart within it be strengthened, and every atmosphere be touched by God's presence. As His word declares, " *Except the Lord build the house, they labour in vain that build it"* (**Psalm 127:1**). When God is invited into our home, He brings order, rest, and quiet assurance. His presence settles anxious thoughts, strengthens weary hearts, and fills ordinary moments with a sense of sacred peace.

Trust that God is able to guard your home and bless all who dwell within it.

Prayer

Lord, bless my home. Let peace rest here and let Your presence shape the atmosphere. Cover every room with Your protection and fill this place with Your love. Let this home be a place of rest, safety, and renewal for all who enter. Guard our hearts, quiet our minds, and let Your peace dwell richly here. May Your presence be felt in both quiet moments and busy days, and may this home reflect Your goodness and care. Amen.

Blessing Declaration

My home is covered in God's peace. His presence dwells where I live.

Personal Declaration (Write Below)

Today, I speak peace and blessings over __________ in my home.

____

____

____

DAY 30

A Whisper of Confidence for the Year Ahead

For the Lord shall be thy confidence and shall keep thy foot from being taken.

Proverbs 3:26

As you close these 30 days, step into the year renewed, strengthened, and covered by the God's blessings. Confidence in God is not loud or rushed it is a steady, quiet assurance rooted in trust. It is the confidence that comes from knowing that God goes before you, walks beside you, and remains faithful behind you. Scripture reminds us, *"The Lord shall go before you; and the God of Israel will be your reward"* (**Isaiah 52:12**). You do not need to have every detail figured out to move forward. When your confidence is anchored in God, you can walk calmly into the unknown, trusting that He has already prepared the way.

> **Confidence Quote for the Year Ahead**
>
> *I step into this year with quiet confidence, trusting the God who goes before me, walks beside me, and holds every day ahead.*

You do not enter this year alone. God's hand rests over your purpose, His peace guards your heart, and His favor directs your steps. **Proverbs 3:26** *The Lord will be your confidence and shall keep your foot from being taken.* Even when the path ahead feels uncertain, His presence remains constant. Walk forward with confidence not in your own strength, but in the One who holds your entire year in His hands. **Psalm 37:5** *Commit thy way unto the Lord; trust also in him; and he shall bring it to pass.* Each step you take is supported by His wisdom, grace, and unfailing care.

Prayer

Lord, be my confidence as I enter this year. Lead me with wisdom, strengthen me when I feel unsure, and bless every step I take. Help me to trust You with what I can see and what I cannot. Quiet my fears, steady my heart, and remind me daily that my life is held securely in Your hands. I step forward with faith, trusting that you are guiding my path and covering my year with Your peace and purpose. Amen.

Blessing Declaration

God is my confidence. I step into this year with peace, purpose, and assurance.

Personal Declaration (**Write Below**)

Today, I step into the year with confidence by choosing to

____

____

____

Closing Reflection

As this journey comes to a close, remember that the end of these pages is not the end of God's work in your life. What you have read, prayed, and declared here was never meant to stay confined to a single season.

The whispers you've listened for of hope, peace, trust, healing, and gratitude are invitations to continue walking closely with God each day. Carry them into your mornings, your decisions, your relationships, and your quiet moments of prayer.

May you move forward with a deeper awareness of God's presence, trusting that he is still guiding you, still blessing you, and still speaking often more softly than expected, but with purpose and love.

Personal Declaration Prayer

Heavenly Father,

I thank You for the words You have placed on my heart throughout this journey. I bring every declaration I have written before You now not as demands, but as expressions of faith and trust in who You are.

Seal these declarations with Your truth. Align my heart with Your will. Strengthen my faith when doubt tries to rise and remind me of these words when I need reassurance.

As I return to these declarations throughout the year, help me remember that You are faithful to complete what You begin. I trust You with every prayer spoken and every hope still unfolding. Amen.

Personal Declaration Chart

Purpose of This Section

This chart was created to help you gather and revisit the declarations you've spoken in faith throughout this devotional. Writing them in one place allows you to reflect pray and recite them as reminders of God's promises and the growth you've experienced over time.

Return to this section whenever you need encouragement. Let these words strengthen your faith, renew your perspective, and remind you of what God has spoken over your life.

Day	
Topic	
Declaration	

Day	
Topic	
Declaration	

Day	
Topic	
Declaration	

Day	
Topic	
Declaration	

Day	
Topic	
Declaration	

Day	
Topic	
Declaration	

Day	
Topic	
Declaration	

Day	
Topic	
Declaration	

Day	
Topic	
Declaration	

Day	
Topic	
Declaration	

Day	
Topic	
Declaration	

Day	
Topic	
Declaration	

Day	
Topic	
Declaration	

Day	
Topic	
Declaration	

Day	
Topic	
Declaration	

Day	
Topic	
Declaration	

Day	
Topic	
Declaration	

Day	
Topic	
Declaration	

Day	
Topic	
Declaration	

Day	
Topic	
Declaration	

Day	
Topic	
Declaration	

Day	
Topic	
Declaration	

Day	
Topic	
Declaration	

Day	
Topic	
Declaration	

Day	
Topic	
Declaration	

Day	
Topic	
Declaration	

Day	
Topic	
Declaration	

Day	
Topic	
Declaration	

Day	
Topic	
Declaration	

Day	
Topic	
Declaration	

Final Blessing

May the God of hope fill you with peace as you trust Him. May your heart remain open to His guidance, even when the path feels quiet. May you recognize His blessings in both the extraordinary and the ordinary.

And as you continue forward, may you always remember God's whispers are never accidental, and His blessings never arrive without purpose.

Continue the Journey

Your journey does not end here.

The whispers you've listened for throughout these pages were never meant to be limited to thirty days. God continues to speak, guide, and bless long after the final page is turned.

If this devotional has encouraged your heart, know that there are more gentle spaces created to help you stay rooted in prayer, scripture and reflection, especially in seasons when life feels busy, uncertain, or quiet.

You are invited to continue your journey though additional devotionals, guided prayers resources, and faith-centered reflections designed to help you:

- Deepen your daily prayer life.
- Grow in trust and spiritual consistency
- Create quiet moments with God in every season
- Reflect, write, and listen for His leading

Each resource is created with the same heart behind Whispers of Blessings, to offer encouragement without pressure, depth without overwhelm, and space to meet God personally.

Scan to Continue the Journey

Scan this code to explore more devotionals, prayers journals, and faith resources.

May you continue to walk forward with confidence, grace, and expectancy, listening for God's whispers and trusting that His blessings are still unfolding.

The journey continues not because the pages go on, but because God does.

Note

Reflections

(This space is intentionally left open for your continued prayers, reflections, and moments of gratitude as the year unfolds.)